# Sur of

# The Soul of America
## Jon Meacham

*Conversation Starters*

# By BookHabits

# Bonus Downloads
*Get Free Books with **Any Purchase** of* Conversation Starters!

Every purchase comes with a FREE download!

*Add spice to any conversation*
*Never run out of things to say*
*Spend time with those you love*

**Get it Now**

or Click Here.

**Scan Your Phone**

**Tips for Using Conversation Starters:**

EVERY GOOD BOOK CONTAINS A WORLD FAR DEEPER THAN the surface of its pages. Questions herein are designed to bring us beneath the surface of the page and invite us into the world that lives on. These questions can be used to:

- Foster a deeper understanding of the book
- Promote an atmosphere of discussion for groups
- Assist in the study of the book, either individually or corporately
- Explore unseen realms of the book as never seen before

# Table of Contents

Introducing *The Soul of America* ............................................................... 6

Discussion Questions ............................................................................. 14

Introducing the Author ........................................................................... 35

Fireside Questions.................................................................................. 42

Quiz Questions ...................................................................................... 53

Quiz Answers......................................................................................... 66

Ways to Continue Your Reading ............................................................. 67

# Introducing *The Soul of America*

BARACK OBAMA, DONALD TRUMP AND HILLARY CLINTON are the names that fill America's newspapers today. The current political climate in America is filled with loyalties, divisions and partisan fury. Pulitzer Prize award-winning biographer Jon Meacham reminds us of the times when America was truly great. In his book *The Soul of America,* Meacham takes us back to the time of the presidents who have gone centuries before Obama and Trump. Meacham says that the great American presidents have overcome the demons of their own time. How did they do so? They summoned "the better angels of our nature". These better angels are the parts of the human's core that is guided by faith and hope. These often result to inclusion and social justice and causes the American people to thrive in spite of the unforgiving circumstances.

Jon Meacham is referring to Abraham Lincoln's speech on March 4, 1861. It was his first inaugural address when he assumed office as the 16th President of the United States. He delivered this iconic speech in front of the unfinished Capitol in Washington, D.C. Here, Lincoln inspired the newly formed confederate states and the country to initiate the restoration of the union. He believed that the American people can grow past the discord and be healed from the wounds if the Americans would commit themselves for the greater good. This domestic camaraderie would only be possible if the American people would be "touched, as surely they will be, by the better angels of our nature." In spite of this inspiring and eloquent words, Abraham Lincoln failed to summon those angels and the divided nation started the war. Jon Meacham says that the American history is a progression of slow and painful steps forward and back. He recalls the times of the other great American presidents like Theodore Roosevelt, Ulysses Grant, Woodrow Wilson, Harry Truman, Franklin Roosevelt, Lyndon Johnson and Dwight Eisenhower. Lyndon B.

Johnson's challenge during his time was the fight against Jim Crow. Johnson ensured that the Civil Rights Act of 1964 will be passed along with the Voting Rights Act of 1965. Johnson rendered all citizens equal regardless of their race. Each of the presidents have gone through the challenges of their own presidency and have overcome the demons of their time.

*The Soul of America* is also filled with stories of the courage of influential American civil rights activists. One of the stories he shared was about the American civil rights activist and Baptist minister Martin Luther King, Jr. He is known for his civil disobedience and non-violence. King credits his tactics to his Christian beliefs and the inspiration of

Mahatma Gandhi's movement in India. Meacham shares his courage alongside other civil rights activists like Rosa Parks. Parks is considered the first lady of civil rights movement. She showed her courage during the Montgomery Bus Boycott when she refused to move. The United States Congress deem Parks as the mother of the freedom movement. Meacham shares the spirit of other notable women in American history. He shares about the courage of suffragettes like Carrie Chapman Catt and Alice Paul who defied the status quo of their time. Catt and Paul were early suffragettes who led an army of women in 1919 to coerce the Congress to give them the right to vote. Their campaign bore fruit a year after when women were given the rights to vote after the ratification of the Nineteenth Amendment to the American constitution.

Meacham also recalls the significant turning points in the history of the United Stated of America. He writes about the American Civil War. This war is a result of the controversy over slavery. This war started shortly after Lincoln delivered his speech about the "better angels." It was a war between the secessionists of the Confederate States against the nationalists of the Union. This, according to Meacham is a significant point in the American history, where Americans showed their unwavering spirit and courage. Meacham also wrote about the First World War and how America became a refuge for immigrants. He followed this with the America First campaign years before the Second World War.

According to Meacham, the struggles then and now is the assertion of hope over fear. He says that the American story have been sustained for centuries because of hope even in the darkest times in history. He believes that Lincoln's better angels will always prevail in the American people.

*Booklist* describes *The Soul of America* an "engrossing, edifying, many-voiced chronicle." *USA Today* praises Meacham's book that it is "thoroughly researched and smoothly written." *Newsday* says that *The Soul of America* is "gripping and inspiring."

# Discussion Questions

*"Get Ready to Enter a New World"*

**Tip:** Begin with questions dealing with broader issues to ensure ample time for quality discussions. Read through all discussion questions before engaging.

## question 1

According to Jon Meacham, the current political climate in America is not new. The loyalties, divisions and partisan fury have been going on for centuries. How does Meacham describe today's political climate? How is it similar to the time of the American fathers?

~ ~ ~

## question 2

Meacham recalls Abraham Lincoln's speech on March 4, 1861. This is his first inaugural address when he assumed office as the 16th President of the United States. According to Meacham, what can we learn from this this speech?

~ ~ ~

## question 3

Lincoln delivered his first inaugural address in Washington. Shortly after his speech, a significant event that was contrary to his words transpired in the other American states. What significant event happened after Lincoln's 1861 speech?

## question 4

The Lost Cause is the literary and intellectual movement in the aftermath of the Civil War. This involves the Southern white society and the confederates. What is the Lost Cause?

~~~

~~~

## question 5

Each of the presidents have gone through the challenges of their own presidency and have overcome the demons of their time. Lyndon Johnson's was the long crusade against Jim Crow. How did Johnson put an end to Jim Crow?

~~~

~~~

## question 6

Martin Luther King Jr. is a Baptist minister. He became a significant figure in the civil rights movement. What is Martin Luther King Jr.'s contribution to the civil rights movement?

~~~

~~~

## question 7

Rosa Parks is most famous for the Montgomery Bus Boycott. She is considered the first lady of the Civil Rights movement. What is the bus situation during Parks's time?

~~~

~ ~ ~

## question 8

Johnson rendered all citizens equal regardless of their race. He ensured that the Congress will pass the laws that will benefit black American citizens. What are the two significant laws passed during Johnson's time?

~ ~ ~

## question 9

Jon Meacham writes about Susan Anthony and her compelling speech at Seneca Falls, New York. Anthony is one of the key figures in the women's suffrage movement. Apart from Anthony, who are the other women suffragettes who led the movement?

~ ~ ~

## question 10

Senator Huey Long and Catholic priest Father Charles Coughlin strongly voiced their concerns about the irrational and unbalanced distribution of wealth and power during the Great Depression. Why are Long and Coughlin considered demagogues?

~ ~ ~

## question 11

Meacham made a comment on today's partisan fury over immigrants. He compared it to Theodore Roosevelt's "melting pot." What are the similarities and differences between today's political climate and Roosevelt's time?

~~~

## question 12

Senator Joseph McCarthy is a Republican Senator who made accusations about the communist party and sympathies to this group. Meacham says that McCarthy's crusade and its opponents are a significant display of the American soul. What is Senator McCarthy's campaign against the communists? According to Meacham, why is it significant?

## question 13

Meacham also cited the Army–McCarthy hearings. These hearings were held in 1954 by the United States Senate's Subcommittee on Investigations. What was the Senate investigating about?

~~~

~~~

## question 14

The Klu Klux Klan had a following of four million members. The Klan was particularly active during the Reconstruction and during the Wilson administration. What was the power of the Klan during its peak? How did the Klan fade?

~~~

~~~

## question 15

Klu Klux Klan was first established in the 1860s. Then it had a resurgence in the late 1910s. How did the Klan resurface in the 1950s?

~~~

~~~

## question 16

*Booklist* describes *The Soul of America* an "engrossing, edifying, many-voiced chronicle." Meacham's essays in his book features the many voices that shaped America. Whose voice resonate to you the most?

~~~

~~~

## question 17

*USA Today* praises Meacham's book that it is "thoroughly researched and smoothly written." They noted Meacham's advice to find our better angels. What are the advices that Meacham gave in his book? Why do we need to find our better angels?

~~~

~ ~ ~

## question 18

*Newsday* says that *The Soul of America* is "gripping and inspiring." Meacham declares his faith in America that the nation can move beyond Trump. What are Meacham's objections on Trump? Why does Americas need to move beyond Trump?

~ ~ ~

~~~

## question 19

Walter Issacson described *The Soul of America* "a profoundly important book." Why is Meacham's book profoundly important? What does his book teach the young generation of Americans?

~~~

~ ~ ~

## question 20

*The New York Times Book Review* praises Meacham as he "summon[s] the better angels by looking back." They cite that Meacham wrote the book because of Donald Trump and the 2017 Charlottesville white nationalist rallies. What period in history is most comparable to the fear and division we see nowadays?

~ ~ ~

# Introducing the Author

JON MEACHAM IS A PROFESSOR, PRESIDENTIAL biographer, *New York Times* bestselling author and historian. Meacham was born and raised in Chattanooga, Tennessee. He attended St. Nicholas School and The McCallie School. In 1991, Meacham earned his bachelor's degree in English Literature from The University of the South in Sewanee, Tennessee. He graduated salutatorian and summa cum laude.

In 1995, Meacham joined the staff of *Newsweek*. He was a writer for the esteemed magazine. Then he served as the Managing Editor of the magazine for eight years. In 2006 up to 2010, Meacham became the Editor-in-Chief of *Newsweek*. Meacham became Random House's Executive Editor and Executive Vice President. He has written articles for *The New York Times Book Review*. He has also written and edited articles for *Time* magazine. While at Random House, Meacham published the books by Al Gore, Clara Bingham, Charles Peters, Mary Soames, John Danforth, among others. Meacham also served in the editorial staff of *The Washington Monthly* and at *The Chattanooga Times*.

Apart from his career in journalism, Meacham has written several books. His books include *Voices in Our Blood: America's Best on the Civil Rights Movement*; *Franklin and Winston: An Intimate Portrait of an Epic Friendship*; *American Gospel: God, the Founding Fathers, and the Making of a Nation; American Lion: Andrew Jackson in the White House. New York: Random House; Thomas Jefferson: The Art of Power; Destiny and Power: The American Odyssey of George Herbert Walker Bush and The Soul of America: The Battle for Our Better Angels.*

His book *American Lion: Andrew Jackson in the White House* won the 2009 Pulitzer Prize for Biography. In this book, Meacham portrayed Andrew Jackson's bravery when he defied the norms of his time and changed Washington and the American nation for good. According to Meacham, Jackson is both beloved and hated. His election in 1828 became the guiding light for the people and American political arena. Jackson showed democracy to the American people and he pacified the fearful hearts of the nation that faced challenging times. Meacham chronicles Jackson's presidency. Meacham drew inspiration from history and the recently uncovered letters and papers. He describes the drama in Jackson's public and private life through his years sitting in the White House.

In 2010, Jon Meacham and Alison Stewart hosted PBS's news program *Need To Know*. Meacham has frequent television appearances in *Morning Joe*, a show in MSNBC. He also appeared in other MSNBC programs, which includes *The 11th Hour with Brian Williams*. He also appeared in the talk show *Real Time with Bill Maher* in HBO.

In 2014, Meacham went back to University of the South. He taught History in his alma mater. He also taught Political Science at Vanderbilt University. Mecham is a strong critic of the current United States president Donald Trump. He has written his strong views against Trump and compared him to Charles Coughlin during The Great Depression. He also made a negative assessment of Trump's manner of speaking and compared it to that of Reagan and Roosevelt. Several universities gave Meacham honorary doctorates. Some of these universities are The University of the South, Dickinson College, Wake Forest University, Loyola University New Orleans,

University of Tennessee, Middlebury College and
University of Massachusetts.

# Bonus Downloads
*Get Free Books with **Any Purchase** of Conversation Starters!*

Every purchase comes with a FREE download!

*Add spice to any conversation*
*Never run out of things to say*
*Spend time with those you love*

**Get it Now**

or Click Here.

**Scan Your Phone**

# Fireside Questions

*"What would you do?"*

**Tip:** These questions can be a fun exercise as it spurs creativity among the readers by allowing alternate scene endings and "if this was you" questions.

## question 21

Meacham is a strong critic of United States president Donald Trump. He compared Trump to Charles Coughlin during The Great Depression. According to Meacham, what are the similarities between Trump and Coughlin?

~ ~ ~

## question 22

According to Meacham's book *American Lion*, Jackson is both beloved and hated. The American people are strongly indebted to his leadership but he advocated some ideas that were unfavorable some. What do the American people love the most about Andrew Jackson? Why is he also hated by some Americans in his day?

~ ~ ~

~ ~ ~

## question 23

Several universities gave Meacham honorary doctorates. Some of these universities are his alma mater The University of the South, Dickinson College and Wake Forest University. How do universities determine who are deserving of honorary doctorates? Why do you think Meacham was awarded several honorary doctorates?

~ ~ ~

## question 24

Meacham received his Pulitzer Prize for his book *American Lion*. Meacham drew inspiration from history and the recently uncovered letters and papers. What can the Americans today learn from the life and presidency of Andrew Jackson?

~~~

~~~

## question 25

Jon Meacham's book *The Soul of America: The Battle for Our Better Angels* recalls the inspiring Lincoln speech. What is Meacham's message to the American people? Why do we need to fight for 'better angels'?

~~~

## question 26

Meacham writes about Senator Huey Long and Rev. Charles Coughlin. He called their move a demagoguery. If you were Reverend Coughlin, would you appear before a large audience and bravely voice your negative opinions? Why or why not?

~~~

~~~

## question 27

Rosa Parks is most famous for her Montgomery Bus incident. Parks is an important figure in the civil rights movement. If you were Parks, would you bravely hold your ground and not move? What were the risks for Parks during that time?

~~~

~ ~ ~

## question 28

Martin Luther King, Jr. is a Baptist minister turned civil rights activist. He was assassinated in 1968. If you were a minister during the time of Martin Luther King's activism, would you also advocate activism? Or will you be silent about the civil rights movement?

~ ~ ~

~~~

## question 29

The Klu Klux Klan has over four million members. It had three resurgences all throughout the history of the American nation. Will you join the Klu Klux Klan? What is the most appealing ideology of the Klan?

~~~

## question 30

Mecham writes about the courage of suffragettes like Carrie Chapman Catt and Alice Paul who defied the status quo of their time. Catt and Paul led an army of women in 1919 to coerce the Congress to give them the right to vote. What was the station of women during Catt and Paul's time? If you were a women in their time, would you join Catt and Paul and fight for your right to vote?

# Quiz Questions

*"Ready to Announce the Winners?"*

**Tip:** Create a leaderboard and track scores to see who gets the most correct answers. Winners required. Prizes optional.

~~~

## quiz question 1

Baptist minister Martin Luther King, Jr. is known for his civil disobedience and non-violence. He protested alongside other civil rights activists. Who is the first lady of the civil rights movement?

~~~

~~~

**quiz question 2**

Senator Huey Long strongly voiced his concerns about the irrational and unbalanced distribution of wealth and power during the Great Depression. Who was the Catholic priest who joined Long in his demagoguery?

~~~

## quiz question 3

The Klu Klux Klan had a following of four million members. The Klan was particularly active during the Wilson administration and resurfaced in the 1950s. What era was the Klan established?

~~~

## quiz question 4

Carrie Chapman Catt defied the status quo of her time. Catt coerced the Congress to give women the right to vote. What part of the American constitution was ratified during this time?

~~~

~~~

## quiz question 5

**True or False:** Jon Meacham recalled Abraham Lincoln's speech on March 4, 1861. It was his first inaugural address when he became President. Abraham Lincoln was the 8th President of the United States.

~~~

~~~

## quiz question 6

**True or False:** Martin Luther King, Jr. is known for his civil disobedience and non-violence. King credits his tactics to his Christian beliefs and the inspiration of Mahatma Gandhi's movement in India.

~~~

## quiz question 7

**True or False:** Coretta Scott is considered the first lady of civil rights movement. As the wife of Martin Luther King, Jr., Scott is recognized by the Congress as the mother of the freedom movement.

## quiz question 8

Jon Meacham earned his bachelor's degree in English Literature from _____. He graduated summa cum laude.

~~~

## quiz question 9

Jon Meacham is a *New York Times* bestselling author and presidential historian. His book _____ won the 2009 Pulitzer Prize for Biography.

~~~

## quiz question 10

In 2014, Jon Meacham went back to University of the South where he taught History. He also taught Political Science at _____.

## quiz question 11

**True or False:** Mecham is a strong critic of Hillary Clinton. He has written his strong views against her and compared her to Charles Coughlin during The Great Depression.

~~~

### quiz question 12

**True or False:** Jon Meacham has been given several awards for his excellence as an author. He received his first Pulitzer award for his book *Voices in Our Blood: America's Best on the Civil Rights Movement.*

# Quiz Answers

1.   Rosa Parks
2.   Father Charles Coughlin
3.   Reconstruction Era
4.   Nineteenth Amendment
5.   False
6.   True
7.   False
8.   The University of the South
9.   American Lion: Andrew Jackson in the White House
10.  Vanderbilt University
11.  False
12.  False

# Ways to Continue Your Reading

EVERY month, our team runs through a wide selection of books to pick the best titles for readers and reading groups, and promotes these titles to our thousands of readers – sometimes with free downloads, sale dates, and additional brochures.

[Click here to sign up for these benefits.](#)

**If you have not yet read the original work or would like to read it again, you can purchase the original book here.**

# Bonus Downloads
*Get Free Books with **Any Purchase** of Conversation Starters!*

Every purchase comes with a FREE download!

***Add spice to any conversation***
***Never run out of things to say***
***Spend time with those you love***

**Get it Now**

or Click Here.

**Scan Your Phone**

# On the Next Page...

If you found this book helpful to your discussions and rate it a 4 or 5, please write us a review on the next page.

*Any* length would be fine but we'd appreciate hearing you more! We'd be very encouraged.

**Till next time,**

**BookHabits**

*"Loving Books is Actually a Habit"*

CPSIA information can be obtained
at www.ICGtesting.com
Printed in the USA
LVHW022253121118
596825LV00006B/356/P